It's a beautiful morning:

An introduction to Japa Yoga as a tool to manage stress, anxiety, addiction, withdrawal, and really crappy days.

By Rick Neubauer

Table of Contents:

Introduction:

The truth is, we are broken, I am broken. If at times we feel as though we are on the mend, or if we feel whole, it is usually through the impact of some outside source, or it may be that we are fixing someone or something else, or that we believe in love for a moment, or are overtaken by some sort of spiritual renaissance. But most of the time we feel broken. We have been through trauma, in and out of the darkness of the actual event or events but lost within the aftermath. In response, we have practiced numbing ourselves with any number of things; exercise, workaholic behavior, addiction to just about anything, and more. We have tried medication, counseling, religion, television, and a host of even less healthy things to glue ourselves back together. That thing: Anger, resentment, fear, anxiety, avoidance, attention seeking, spending half your life trying to forget what happened, and the other half trying to remember. You ride the tides of productive behavior or prolonged rest, or you hold your breath through the panic attack and spend the rest of the time waiting for the next one. There are times in between when you are nothing but numb. You overachieve for a time, then step back and isolate. When everyone else wants to get ahead, you create your own rationale for staying in the same place. Material things mean almost nothing, or they mean everything. Goals? Well you build upon nothing, for every foundation seems flawed. You learn about forgiveness, and even practice it at a novice level. If you go to a support group, forgiveness is talked about, but to you, some things are unforgivable. You pretend that you have dealt with it. The grass is always greener on the other side, or so you make yourself believe that it is. Most people you know are screwed up. You don't spend much time talking about the subject, and if you find someone else to whom this terror has happened, you don't need to say a word. They understand you and you understand them, even if you are from different planets.

Love has many meanings, which you come to know in hundreds of temporary ways, from the romantic kiss on a moonlit pier, to the bondage of your arms against the bedpost in the middle of the day. Love can be a briefly shared cup of coffee staring into a pair of eyes, or the hand held by a person in need as you listen intently. It can be the love of a favorite baseball team, or the love of angry advocacy for a population or cause embraced by almost no one else, for being this way, it is easy to believe in and fight for a minority cause. And there are those who just love to fight, for it releases, if only for a short time, the pent-up tension. The same tension you sought to release when you cut or tatted your own skin, perhaps during a time of numbness. When someone hurts you this way it feels like you may never heal, like it will never go away. Sometimes it is way in the back of your mind, sometimes it is so close to the front that your head hurts, your breathing quickens, your hands clench, and you sweat. You have tension, there is that word again, in your shoulders, in your back, and the rest is just a pain in the ass. You run, maybe you run towards or run away, but you run. You try religion, art, counseling, vegetarian diets, travel, and some less wholesome approaches to stress management, but ultimately there must be love. There needs to be love, no matter how brief, for there needs to be something better than what is during the times of no love at all. Love can mean you need someone, or want someone, or like someone. It can also mean "please don't leave me" or "I have no place else to go". You wonder all of the time how long love will last, or how long anything will last. So, who will you grow old with? Someone who knows, or someone who doesn't know. Do you actually believe that it is possible to explain to another human being what happened? That they might feel okay holding you, skin against skin. A skin that takes a lifetime to feel comfortable in afterwards. So perhaps you say nothing, and the rest of the time is just filling in the gaps. Or maybe you don't need to explain, which is always a bargain, and rare. You are rare. Or maybe there is just anger, resentment, fear, anxiety, avoidance, attention seeking, spending half your life trying to forget what happened, and the other half trying to remember. What you read in the following pages might not be the answer for you. It is something else, and that may be a compass that points you in the right direction. That is my hope that maybe there is some glue here to hold you together.

Compasses:

Often, there is an event, or a chain of events, that are so traumatic, so painful that a person must leave the physical location where the events occurred. For others, the normal process of growing up and differentiation from parents and siblings causes us to move on. Still for others it is a career, or marriage, that prompts relocation. But whatever it is that causes us to leave the place we once called home, along the roadways, or skyways or seaways, we often get lost. There are so many ways to get lost, pcoplc, placcs, and things to gct lost within. Jobs, hobbies, friends, relationships, parenthood, volunteer work, a taste of success, a pair of eyes, a touch of silk, a hint of aloneness, or the visual and auditory noise of chaos. These things take us from where we are headed and render us almost completely disoriented, lost, at least for a little while. If we are persistent, if we know who we really are, and where we wanted to go all along, we find our way again. We find, or create new homes, reshaping them, and sometimes working from the plan right inside of ourselves. But getting there again requires help. I was lost. Several times I was lost. Yet, throughout my journey I carried many compasses. I carried a compass my father had given to me. I carried a rosary too, one that my grandmother prayed with. I carried books, Steinbeck, Hemingway, Baudelaire, Good News for Modern Man", I ran, and I practiced japa yoga. I practiced until I was lost, and found my way again. Nothing in life, a life worth living, is ever very simple. Yet somehow, our compasses can guide us home.

In the middle of the river:

My friend Michael once told me of a Gestalt therapy weekend course that he once attended, where they spent eight hours each day standing in the river. He joked that he wished he had taken his fishing pole but said most of the weekend was about being aware of what was happening in the here and now, not focusing on the past, not focusing on the future. "Don't push the river", was the quote, "it will flow by itself". Gestalt does not translate easily from the native German, but in the best translation it means "glued together". We spend some time in this life falling apart, so it seems we should also spend some real time trying to figure out what keeps us glued together.

Instead of starting at the beginning, let's begin in the middle.

Circle what applies:
Upsetting dreams or nightmares.

Avoiding places or topics of discussion.

Negative thoughts about yourself, other people or the world.

Difficulty maintaining close relationships.

Feeling detached from family and friends.

Lack of interest in activities you once enjoyed.

Feeling emotionally numb.

Being easily startled or frightened.

Trouble sleeping.

Trouble concentrating or focusing.

Irritability, angry outbursts or aggressive behavior.

Overwhelming guilt or shame.

Restlessness.

Panic attacks.

Agitation.

Insomnia.

Muscle tension or soreness.

Shaking or tremor.

Fast heartbeat.

Rapid breathing.

Sometimes twisting thoughts in your mind.

Hyperactivity or hypersensitivity.

Mood swings.

Please put your pencil down for a minute.

Much of what is listed here includes what happens to our bodies or mind post trauma. Many of these symptoms also occur in withdrawal from opioid addiction, alcohol or Benzodiazepine addiction, gambling or sex addiction, or stressful changes in life. The degree to which they occur or the frequency of which they occur is something to pay attention to. We all experience sadness or guilt sometimes, but it does not necessarily affect every choice we make or the tasks of our daily living. Withdrawal is defined as the combination of physical and mental effects that a person experiences after they stop using or reduce their intake of a substance such as alcohol and prescription or recreational drugs. PTSD or mood disorders are the presence of a combination of symptoms over a period of time, which interfere with the activities of daily living. End as beginning: We need a clean mind and a clean body So that our hearts can work the way they are supposed to work. Let's assume that you have a pretty good collection of the signs and symptoms listed above. You may try to lasso in one or two, for example most people seek counseling or medication for prolonged anxiety, or you may try to ignore the symptoms altogether. If you look carefully at the list, most of the items fall into two categories: Things that are happening with the body Things that are happening inside the head. There is the strange overlap in anxiety, for example the thought that you could be harmed, resulting in muscle tension, gastrointestinal distress, followed by irritability, restlessness, or the inability to sleep. So, the focus of this technique is to master the mind before the thoughts have a chance to settle into the body. We won't always be successful, so then we need to work on that too.

It's a beautiful morning:

Did you ever wake up with a song playing in your head? Or you are driving down the highway and suddenly for no reason, you begin singing a favorite song? Of course, we all have. This is your brain telling you something. Pay attention! A song, a prayer, a mantra, an affirmation, a poem, making mental lists of things that you are grateful for, repeating anything for as little as fifteen minutes a day can calm the mind, help focus and attend to task, relax the body, and help you overcome a world of challenges. We are what we think, and choosing a phrase to think about daily can be the cornerstone to better physical and mental health. A study by Gemma Perry in Australia, found that chanting can decrease stress, anxiety and depressive symptoms, as well as increase positive mood, feelings of relaxation and focused attention, Sarah Warren, clinical somatics practitioner and researcher, reports that making a list of things we are grateful for seems to be directly protective against stress and depression, and retrains the brain. There is also support that people who express gratitude are happier and less likely to develop or continue addictive behaviors. Every faith and denomination within that faith has a collection of prayers. A study completed in China reports that repeating phrases makes a difference when managing pain and can decrease opioid withdrawal symptoms. We all know the story of the Little Engine that Could. I started with a song from the Rascals and sang it every morning. "It's a beautiful morning" was the song I sang in my head, and then suddenly, it was there. It was there when I wanted it, and there when I needed it. I have moved on to other things, but that is where I started.

It is hard to get unstuck and move forward, but we must practice. So, what if you picked a poem, or prayer, or mantra, and said it somewhere between 600 and 700 times a day? Not all of the time, but for the first four or five days of practice. Then the brain has it, and when you need it, you can easily return to it. Perhaps you have a series of unplanned evenings, or sleepless nights, or vacation or sick days. That would be a good way to begin. After that, refresher of fifteen minutes a day can keep you going strong. That may be as little as your daily commute to work, or your grooming time. People say they want to lose weight, or stop having panic attacks, or cease their drug addiction, or be a better employee. People say a lot of things. I spent years as a clinician in mental health centers teaching people progressive muscle relaxation. It is a simple clinical skill that the American Psychiatric Association, the American and Canadian Counseling Associations, and the Australian Association for Behavior Analysis all agree is a key to managing anxiety, eliminate panic attacks, and better manage pain. In all of the years I trained patients and clients to do the technique, I can count on my hands the ones who committed to it. Most thought the pain or panic would pass, or that it could be managed through medication, setting forth little effort into real self-change.

Abhyasa

In the Yoga Sutras, abhyasa is discussed as a combination of action and effort. It is the positive path of practice, focused, over a long time. In other words, it is constant and continuous practice. Our brains get bored, and if we do not put healthy thoughts into them, they create their own thoughts, sometimes wholly distorted, often unhealthy thoughts. In fact, Anxiety itself is a physical manifestation of a thought. It is said that 80% of us will be challenged by anxiety at some point in our lives. Whether it be post-trauma, mid-recovery, deep withdrawal, or fatigue at the end of a long, chaotic day, it is important to control the mind to the best of our ability. I chose a song first, and then a daily mantra, and in the words of Robert Frost, that has made all the difference. How will you choose your phrase or mantra? It may align with your values, or it may be something

entirely new to you, but remember:
Abhyasa.

Sensorimotor Patterning

At a large psychiatric center on a hill, the first doctor I ever worked with, Dr Grey said "move everything every day". It was a far cry from yoga but gave me a healthy respect for the connection between physical movement and mental health. Just a few years later, my body stretched out on the floor, I wondered what to do. My back was shattered, my hips displaced, my left foot had lost all feeling and motor control and dragged behind me when I walked. Running, which I had used for my physical and mental health, was not an option. Any movement would be welcomed, but every movement hurt, a deep, burning, grinding, intense pain.
  When we are young, we move spontaneously, as a way to explore our bodies and the world in general. These developmental patterns (lifting your head, crawling, rolling, etc.) not only help us gently move, but they are very much the

core of yoga and somatic strategies that address pain and discomfort. Remember rolling down a hill as a child? You laughed, and let gravity take your body. I had forgotten and could not imagine that. After weeks of physical therapy, I hurt even more. I was raised on the lyrics of Paul Simon and Janis Ian, so I knew life would be tough, but I was also raised on the words of Pete Seeger, so I knew there was hope.   Hope came in the form of a Vietnam veteran, who was once strapped to a stretcher on a helicopter under fire. The Huey Cobra took off, but the stretcher, not strapped in, came loose, dropping the soldier from the air to the ground.   He spent years managing pain, before he trained himself to overcome it. To train a body to breathe into and through areas of tension or pain takes practice. Notice that you breathe shallow when in pain or having a panic attack, and that needs to change. To add movement to this miracle breath is the beginning of yoga. Yoga asanas were never intended to be done quickly, rather with precision and in rock steady fashion. Breathing helps to deepen a pose, or release tension while holding a pose, or allow the body to relax, and during any given pose, several different breathing techniques may be used. I learned two asanas (or poses) in two years, which makes me chuckle when I think of the current state of yoga classes. The last time I attended a studio, the instructor covered 27 poses in 55 minutes, in what was identified as an introduction to yoga. In neuro-developmental therapy, they talk about elongating one set of muscles, while shortening the opposite side. In sensory motor treatment, they discuss the balance between facilitation and inhibition of opposing muscle groups. So, I took my two yoga poses on the road. I practiced them, not only on the floor, but when walking, when sitting, when stretched over the handlebars on a bike. My two poses or asanas, in fact all efficient movement patterns, begin with breath, and motion initiated at the base of the Spine. Bill, my instructor, learned yoga over twenty years before he shared his teachings with me. I practiced yoga for over thirty years before I searched for a program through which to become a teacher. I had written to the Yoga Alliance and Yoga Journal when certification first was being considered. I expressed my concern that a two-hundred, or five-a hundred-hour course was not near enough to train quality yoga instructors. I eventually went on to become certified, but it turns out that I was correct; that too many people are out there sharing misinformation. Since I cannot fix that, I focused on my practice, and my journey alone.   I am forever in gratitude to Bill. Through Mary Irby, a tremendous yoga instructor, I have learned that we define our own yoga practice over time. She shared with me the story of a woman she met in India, who simply chose one asana to practice multiple times daily, and grew older, most gracefully. Again, it is abhyasa, the positive path of practice, focused, over a long time. In other words, it is constant and continuous practice. Through these practices, one can control and release tension in the body, and rewire the brain to allow healing.   Note: The control of a body part, with proper breathing, can occur with most forms of movement. Pilates, high intensity training, Qigong, weightlifting, boxing, all of these can provide the same benefit if focus is placed on the motion and breath.

And in the end…

      This is the real world. We are real people. This is real life, and things sometimes happen that don't fit in with how we think the story should go. Digging out of holes takes time and is sometimes a matter of perception. There is an old story of six blind men who went to see an elephant. Because they were blind, and much smaller than the gigantic beast, they each explored a different part of the elephant. Therefore, each proudly announced that he knew what an elephant was, simply by feeling and describing the one part of the animal they experienced. We do this all of the time, seldom seeing the entire picture. We see a minute of the movie, and believe we know the whole story. Sometimes it seems like the best we can do is to practice every day, to try to rest or untwist our minds and our bodies, so that our hearts work the way they are supposed to. In recovery, be it from traumatic events, focused on mental health, or including addiction, there are stages that occur. Being honest with yourself is key, but difficult, because you are dealing with difficult things. If something easy would have worked, it would have already worked. Other steps include practicing self-care, reaching out to others, and asking for help. Almost every approach to mental health and recovery includes some form of body-mind relaxation. There are plenty of them out there, and this is just one such option. I am hopeful that you have found these pages worth your while, if not for concrete ideas that work, at least for distraction from the pain. I am also hopeful that today, for you, is better than yesterday.

Appendix, or Plug into love:

   We would like to believe that love is
without conditions. That no matter how our
friends or parents or partners behave, that
we would love them and they would love us.
But they don't make it easy, do they? Qi, or
prana, is the circulating life energy that is
thought to be inherent in all living things.
Love is inherent in all living things. So,
imagine we view love as a sort of energy.
We plug in something that needs energy,
and it works. We fill our car with energy and
it goes. We fill our fireplace with energy and
it heats. What if we plugged ourselves into
love? If we could view love as energy, the
good stuff, then we could go. We could feel
better, we could heal, we could connect with
others and they would feel better. We could
live in the present moment filled with love.
We could undo self-inflicted pain and feel
better. We could be, what is that word,
happy? The love is inside of you, flowing

like electricity, waiting to be tapped. Forget about yesterday, forget about bad, right now there is love. Pain, hurt, anger, sadness, they do not matter as much as love. Love every day. There are so many things to love. Think only about love, start now.

Made in the USA
Columbia, SC
20 November 2023

26524012R00017